THE
ULTIMATE
Lullaby
COLLECTION

Twin Sisters Productions, LLC
4710 Hudson Drive, Stow, OH 44224 USA
www.twinsisters.com   1-800-248-8946

ISBN-13: 978-159922-336-0

Name: _____

Birthdate / Time: _____

Weight: _____

Length: _____

Hospital: _____

Doctor: _____

Those attending the birth: _____

_____

Special delivery ♡

Our journey begins

FIRST pictures

Our little miracle...

...our baby sent from heaven.

Brahms' Lullaby

Lullaby and good night,
With roses delight,
With lilies bespread
Is baby's wee bed.

Lay thee down now and rest;
May thy slumber be blessed.
Lay thee down now and rest;
May thy slumber be blessed.

Lullaby and good night,
Thy mother's delight,
Bright angels around
My darling shall stand.

They will guard thee from harms;
Thou shalt wake in my arms.
They will guard thee from harms;
Thou shalt wake in my arms.

It's Night-Night Time

It's night-night time, night-night time,
Lay your head on me.
It's night-night time, night-night time
Time to go to sleep.
I'll sing to you and hold you close.
It's night-night time, night-night time.
Time to go to sleep.

It's night-night time, night-night time,
In your crib you go.
It's night-night time, night-night time
Mommy loves you so.
I'll sing to you while you close your eyes.
It's night-night time, night-night time.
Mommy loves you so.

Rock-A-Bye Baby

Rock-a-bye Baby, on the treetop,
When the wind blows the cradle will rock.
When the bow breaks, the cradle will fall
And down will come baby, cradle and all.

One
Month
Old

All Through The Night

Sleep, my child, and peace attend thee
All through the night.
Guardian angels God will send thee
All through the night.
Soft the drowsy hours are creeping,
Hill and dale in slumber sleeping.
I my loving vigil keeping,
All through the night.

While the moon her watch is keeping
All through the night.
While the weary world is sleeping
All through the night.
O'er thy spirit gently stealing,
Visions of delight revealing.
Breathes a pure and holy feeling,
All through the night.

Golden Slumbers

Golden slumbers kiss your eyes;
Smiles awake you when you rise.
Sleep, pretty darlings do not cry,
And I will sing a lullaby.
Rock them, rock them, lullaby.

Care is heavy, therefore sleep you.
You are care and care must keep you.
Sleep, pretty darlings, do not cry,
And I will sing a lullaby.
Rock them, rock them, lullaby.

Two Months Old

Raindrops

Raindrops a-falling from the skies;
Tired and sleepy, close your eyes.
Tired and sleepy while the skies
  are weeping,
Weeping and singing you their lullabies.
Tired and sleepy, while the skies
  are weeping,
Weeping and singing you their lullabies.

Go To Sleep, Little One

Go to sleep.
Go to sleep, sleep, sleep.
Go to sleep, little one.
Close your eyes and dream tender dreams
For you are guarded, protected by my love.
Now, go to sleep.
Go to sleep, sleep, sleep.
Go to sleep, little one.
Close your eyes and dream tender dreams
For you are guarded, protected by my love.

Long have I waited; I've waited for you.
Go to sleep.
Years I spent hoping and praying for you.
Go to sleep.
Now that I have you right here by my side,
I will not ever, no, never let you go.

Go to sleep.
Go to sleep, sleep, sleep.
Go to sleep, little one.
Close your eyes and dream tender dreams
For you are guarded, protected by my love.

Three Months Old

At 3 months you...

_____

_____

_____

_____

_____

Your favorite thing to do was...

_____

_____

_____

_____

_____

Sou Gan

Sleep, my baby, on my bosom,
Warm and cozy it will prove.
Round thee mother's arms are folding;
In her heart a mother's love.
There shall no one come to harm thee,
Naught shall break thy rest.
Sleep my darling babe in quiet,
Sleep on mother's gentle breast.

Raisins And Almonds

To my little one's cradle in the night,
Comes a little goat snowy and white.
The goat will trot to the market
While mother her watch does keep,
Bringing back raisins and almonds.
Sleep, my little one, sleep.

Now The Day Is Over

Now the day is over.
Night is drawing nigh.
Shadows of the evening
Steal across the sky.

Bye, Baby Bunting

Bye, baby bunting,
Daddy's gone a-hunting
To get a little rabbit skin
To wrap his baby bunting in.

Four Months Old

Baby Love

Sleep, Baby Sleep

Sleep, baby sleep.
The father guards the sheep.
Thy mother shakes the dreamland tree,
Down falls a little dream for thee.
Sleep, baby sleep.
Sleep, baby sleep.

Sleep, baby sleep.
The father watches the sheep.
The wind is blowing fierce and wild;
It must not wake my little child.
Sleep, baby sleep.
Sleep, baby sleep.

Sleep, baby sleep.
The large stars are the sheep.
The little stars are the lambs, I guess.
The gentle moon's the shepherdess.
Sleep, baby sleep.
Sleep, baby sleep.

Rockin'

Little baby, sweetly sleep, do not weep;
Sleep in comfort, slumber deep.
I will rock you, rock you, rock you.
I will rock you, rock you, rock you.
Little baby, sweetly sleep.
Sleep in comfort, slumber deep.

Fingers And Toes

I'm counting your fingers
    and loving you so;
I'm tickling you gently on each little toe.
I'm singing so sweetly and
    snuggling you close.
I'm kissing you on your nose.
Fingers and toes and where is your nose?
Snuggling and loving, yes,
    that's how it goes.
Hush now, my baby, don't make a peep.
Daddy is trying to put you to sleep.

5 month olds are so special. I love it when you...

_____

_____

_____

_____

_____

Five Months Old

Go To Sleep

Go to sleep, my sweet little brother,
Go to sleep and you'll have a treat.
Go to sleep, my sweet little brother,
Go to sleep and you'll have a treat.
Mama makes a cake.
It's ready to bake.
Papa's down below
And he's making cocoa.
Go to sleep, my sweet little brother,
Go to sleep, my sweet little one.

Go to sleep, my sweet little sister,
Go to sleep and you'll have a treat.
Go to sleep, my sweet little sister,
Go to sleep and you'll have a treat.
Mama makes a cake.
It's ready to bake.
Papa's down below
And he's making cocoa.
Go to sleep, my sweet little sister,
Go to sleep, my sweet little one.

Twinkle, Twinkle Little Star

Twinkle, twinkle little star,
How I wonder what you are.
Up above the world so high
Like a diamond in the sky.
Twinkle, twinkle little star,
How I wonder what you are.

In the dark blue sky you keep,
Often through my curtains peep.
For you never shut your eye,
Till the sun is in the sky.
Twinkle, twinkle little star,
How I wonder what you are.

Six
Months
Old

Love Bug

Dance To Your Daddy

Dance to your daddy, my little baby.
Dance to your daddy, my little lamb.
You shall have a fish and you shall have a fin,
And you shall have a haddock
    when the boat comes in.

Dance to your daddy, my little laddie.
Dance to your daddy, my little man.
You shall have a fishy in a little dishy.
You shall have a haddock
    when the boat comes in.

Mammy Loves

Mammy loves and pappy loves
And mammy loves her little baby.
Go to sleepy, go to sleep.
Go to sleep, you little baby.

Mozart's Lullaby

Sleep, little one, go to sleep.

So peaceful the birds and the sheep.

Quiet are meadows and trees,

Even the buzz of the bees,

The silvery moonbeams so bright,

Down through the window give light.

O'er you the moonbeams will creep,

Sleep, little one, go to sleep.

Good night.

Good night.

All The Pretty Little Horses

Hush-a-bye, don't you cry,
Go to sleepy, little baby.
When you wake, you shall have
All the pretty little horses.
Blacks and bays, dapples and grays,
Coach and six little horses.

Down in the meadow
Lies a poor little lambie.
Bees and butterflies pickin' on its eyes.
Poor little thing is cryin' Mammy.
Blacks and bays, dapples and grays,
Coach and six little horses.

Baby's First...

Christmas

Steps

Baby & Me

Baby & Me

Armenian Lullaby

Sleep, my little one,
My loved one,
As I rock and sing,
As the bright moon watches o'er us,
O'er your little crib.

All Night, All Day

All night, all day,
Angels watching over me, my Lord.
All night, all day,
Angels watching over me.
When at night I go to sleep,
Angels watching over me, my Lord.
Pray the Lord my soul to keep,
Angels watching over me.

The Sandman Comes

The Sandman comes.
The Sandman comes.
He brings such pretty snow white sand
For every child throughout the land.
The Sandman comes.

Seven Months Old

Hush, Little Baby

Hush, little baby, don't say a word,
Mama's gonna buy you a mockingbird.
And if that mockingbird don't sing,
Mama's going to buy you a diamond ring.
If that diamond ring turns brass,
Mama's going to buy you a looking glass.
And if that looking glass get's broke,
Mama's going to buy you a billy goat.
If that billy goat won't pull,
Mama's going to buy you a cart and bull.
And if that cart and bull turns over,
Mama's going to buy you a dog named Rover.
If that dog named Rover don't bark,
Mama's going to buy you a horse and cart.
And if that horse and cart falls down,
You'll still be the sweetest little baby in town.

Eight Months Old

Nine Months Old

Favorite Food:_____

_____

_____

Favorite Toy:_____

_____

_____

Favorite Song:_____

_____

_____

Favorite Thing To Do:_____

_____

_____

What a blessing to watch you grow. At 9 months you...

_____

_____

_____

_____

Ten Months Old

Love you so much!

Eleven Months Old

1 year!

Milestones: _____

_____

_____

_____

_____

_____

_____

_____

_____

_____

_____

_____

A Year In Review

In _____, you:

○ _____

○ _____

○ _____

○ Smiled at me when I told you how much I love you

○ _____

○ _____

○ _____

○ Received over a thousand hugs and kisses